Presented to

_____

by

_____

on

_____

Why did Jesus have to die?

This is a wonderful book, factual, well-illustrated and a great read...highly recommended. *Pastor Chris Gill - King's Church Gillingham*

It's helped me understand why Jesus died even more; the book had beautiful illustrations and it was easy to read and understand. *Joel, age 8*

I love the fact that the book is interactive. *Enam, age 9*

I learnt quite a lot from the book. I liked how it gave relatable examples to explain hard sentences/information, which were tricky to understand. *Ivan, age 10*

Scripture Quotations:
(1) Scripture taken from the New King James Version®. Copyright © 1982 by Thomas Nelson. Used by permission. All rights reserved.
(2) Holy Bible, New International Version®, NIV® Copyright ©1973, 1978, 1984, 2011 by Biblica, Inc.® Used by permission. All rights reserved worldwide.

ACKNOWLEDGEMENTS

I just want to say "thank you" to my pastor – Pastor Chris Gill – who reviewed the manuscript and provided invaluable insights. To my family, for supporting me in writing this up, and especially to my children – Dede and David – for helping me with the illustrations. You guys are amazing!

And most of all, to my Father – thank you, *Abba*.

– *AK*

DEDICATION

To all those asking big questions.

What is this book all about?

As you learn more about the Bible, you are likely to have questions.
Big questions!

One of the questions that most children your age usually ask is "*Why did Jesus have to die?*"

And that's a very good question – understanding why Jesus had to die is at the core of the Christian faith.

This book is written especially with you in mind – to help you find the answer to this question. The question is answered with simplicity and real-life scenarios that will help you grasp the real meaning behind why Jesus had to die.

I hope that this book will become a great aid in helping you grow in your relationship with God. And once you understand this question, don't hesitate to share the same truth with others who are asking the same question.

God bless you.

– Afia Keteku

Imagine someone stole your candy!

The candy you love more than any other candy in the world.

Would it be okay if the person simply said "sorry"?

Now imagine someone has scribbled all over the class register.

The teacher is demanding to know who did it. One of your

classmates says you did it, even though you didn't. You protest

but the teacher does not believe you, and because the teacher

thinks you did scribble over the register (and now thinks you're lying),

you have to apologise in front of the whole class.

You also lose fifteen minutes of playtime.

...After some investigation, the truth is discovered. It turns out the

classmate who lied about you was in fact the one who scribbled over

the class register. For one whole week, they got away with lying about

you and you have had a pretty miserable week. Nobody even wanted to

play with you.

Would you forgive your classmate if they simply said "sorry" to you?

_____

Do you think they should apologise only to you or in front of the whole class?

_____

Do you think your classmate should face other consequences for their behaviour? If so, what might those consequences be?

_____

_____

Are there times when you think just saying "sorry" is not enough?

_____

Most of us would agree that saying "sorry" when we've done something wrong is the right thing to do. If we're the person that was hurt, we might also say, sometimes, saying "sorry" is not enough. There have to be further consequences.

And that is exactly why we are going to explore the question, "Why did Jesus have to die?"

You see, after God created the world and everything in it, He created the first man who was called Adam. He also made the first woman called Eve. God's plan for these first two people was that they would *"be fruitful and multiply; fill the earth and subdue it; have dominion over the fish of the sea, over the birds of the air, and over every living thing that moves on the earth."* (Genesis 1:28 NKJV).

But with great power comes great responsibility, and just as God gave

Adam and Eve authority over every living thing and the entire earth, He

also gave them the great responsibility of looking after the Garden of

Eden. For their hard work of looking after the garden, they could eat

from every tree in the garden apart from the Tree of the Knowledge of

Good and Evil. God said to them, "*...in the day that you eat of it you

shall surely die.*" (Genesis 2:17 NKJV).

The 'death' God referred to was in two ways – there was physical death.

And there was spiritual death, where because they had chosen to go

their own way, they would be separated from God forever. They would

have no relationship with the One who made them and who brought

meaning and purpose to their lives.

Think about this – would a branch survive if it is cut from a tree?

Of course, it wouldn't because it is no longer attached to its source.

That was the same thing that happened when Adam and Eve chose to

disobey God and eat from the tree they had been forbidden to eat

from.

Adam and Eve realised how foolish they had been but saying "sorry"

was not enough. Just like your classmate who probably didn't get away

just by saying "sorry", physical death was the result of Adam and Eve's

sin no matter how sorry they were.

Adam, Eve and all their descendants should have died spiritually too and lost their relationship with God forever. Except that because God is loving and merciful, He provided a way for people to show how sorry they really were so that they could mend their relationship with Him. God instructed them to use blood to atone for their sin. In Leviticus chapter 17 verse 11, God told the Israelites, "*For the life of a creature is in the blood, and I have given it to you to make atonement for yourselves on the altar; it is the blood that makes atonement for one's life.*" (NIV)

To 'atone' for something means to make up or to pay for something or to put that thing right.

Why blood?

Before we answer that question, write down what you think are the main functions of blood in our bodies.

_____

_____

_____

_____

Blood is important to us as human beings. Our hearts pump blood all around our bodies so that nutrients and oxygen are sent to every organ. Blood also removes unwanted materials such as carbon dioxide and germs from our bodies so that we can stay healthy. If a person is wounded and loses lots of blood, they could die. That is why injured people sometimes have blood transfusions so that they can receive the oxygen they need to keep them alive. A person's life *is* in their blood.

Because the consequence of sin was death as we saw in Genesis 2 verse

17, Adam and Eve could only make up for their sin if someone or

something died. More importantly, through dying, that person or thing

would have to lose or shed their blood. Since blood is the substance

that holds life, spilling one's blood was required to prove that the

person or thing had indeed died.

So, Adam and Eve had sinned, right? Who or what do you think had to die so that their blood could atone for Adam and Eve's sin?

_____

If you said they had to die to atone for their own sin, you would probably be right. But think about this for a moment.

If someone had stolen a candy from you and then offered you half a candy to make up, would you accept it?

_____

What about if someone stained your cleanest dress or shirt and offered a dirty one as a replacement? How would you feel?

_____

Very few of us, if any at all, would accept a less-than-perfect replacement for something valuable to us. Most of us would expect a replacement that is as good as, or better than, what we lost.

Because Adam and Eve had sinned and made themselves dirty, they could not die to save themselves. They were less than perfect and nothing they could do was enough to make up for their sin. There had to be another way.

As a temporary solution, God allowed the Israelites to sacrifice animals and use the blood of the animals to make up for their sins (Leviticus chapter 4).

These animals could be bulls, sheep, or goats but they all had to be healthy, clean, and in good condition. Whenever a person sinned, they could only ask for forgiveness when they killed an animal and spilled its blood.

Why were animal sacrifices a temporary solution and why did Jesus still have to die?

Well, you know that dress or shirt that you really love? Maybe you love it because it's in your favourite colour. Or perhaps because it's covered in glitter and stars and sequins. Someone messed it up and they are offering you a replacement. Unlike the dirty replacement in our earlier example, this is a clean new item of clothing...but it doesn't have the glitter, stars or sequins and it's not in your favourite colour.

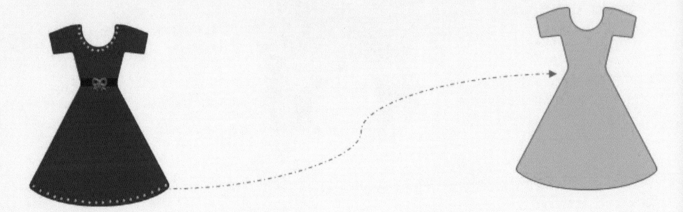

Would you take it?

_____

Even if you took it, would you still insist that you have your perfect item of clothing back?

_____

Sacrificing animals was like offering that clean new item of clothing as a replacement. Animals were okay...but they were not perfect. Here are some of the reasons why:

A human being is superior to an animal. Do you remember how we said earlier on that most of us would only accept a replacement that was as good as, or better than, what we had lost? When a human being sinned, it was only good that another human being died to atone for the sin. Even better, the human being who would die should be a perfect human being who had never done anything wrong.

People had to sacrifice animals whenever they realised they had sinned. Also, every year, the high priest had to sacrifice animals as a pardon for the entire nation. These continual animal sacrifices reminded the people that the blood of animals could never remove the effects of sin completely. Hebrews 10 verses 3 - 4 says that "*But in those sacrifices, there is a reminder of sins every year. For it is not possible that the blood of bulls and of goats should take away sins.*" (NKJV)

People fell into the habit of sacrificing animals without really being sorry for their sins. They began to think that they could sin as long as they sacrificed an animal afterwards.

At the right time, God provided the perfect person who would die in place of sinful people. **This person was Jesus.**

Why was Jesus the perfect sacrifice?

Because by being born of Mary, He was human. And yet because He was also fully God, He lived without sin. Hebrews 4:15 (NIV) says: "*For we do not have a high priest who is unable to empathize with our weaknesses, but we have one who has been tempted in every way, just as we are—yet he did not sin.*" Jesus is the only one who was able to die in our place to make up for the consequence of our sin.

Jesus is the perfect sacrifice because, unlike animals which had to be sacrificed repeatedly, Jesus died once and for all.

Hebrews 10:11-14 says *"Day after day every priest stands and performs his religious duties; again and again he offers the same sacrifices, which can never take away sins. But when this priest had offered for all time one sacrifice for sins, he sat down at the right hand of God, and since that time he waits for his enemies to be made his footstool. For by one sacrifice, he has made perfect forever those who are being made holy."* (NIV)

Through his death, Jesus paid the ultimate cost of sin. Nothing was ever good enough to atone for sin, apart from the blood of another human being – a righteous person in the form of Jesus. No gold, silver or animals would ever pay the ultimate price of sin.

1 Peter 1 verses 18 to 19 puts it this way, "*For you know that it was not with perishable things such as silver or gold that you were redeemed from the empty way of life handed down to you from your ancestors, but with the precious blood of Christ, a lamb without blemish or defect.*" (NIV)

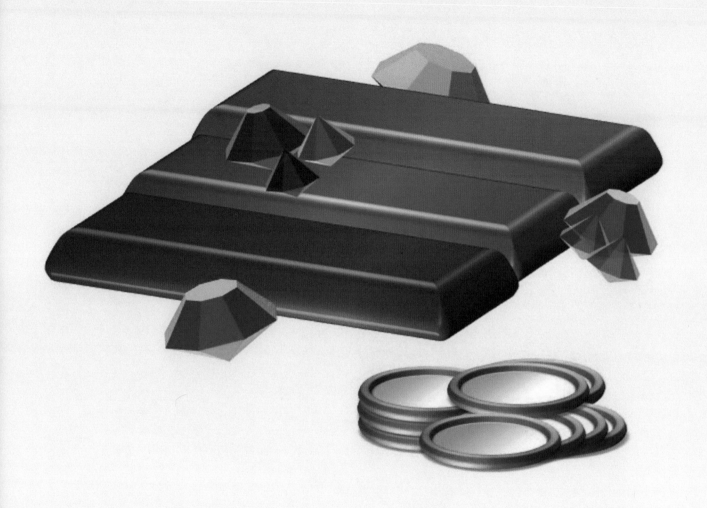

The law demands that we die because we broke God's law.

Romans 6:23 says, "*For the wages of sin is death, but the gift of God is eternal life in Christ Jesus our Lord.*" (NKJV)

Through the death of Jesus, we who accept that He died in our place have also died – we have paid the price of sin. The law demands blood to atone for sins - Jesus bled on the cross so that we can be made clean. Unlike the blood of animals which only showed outward repentance, the blood of Jesus cleans us both on the outside and on the inside.

As Hebrews 9 verses 12 to 13 says, "*The blood of goats and bulls and the ashes of a heifer sprinkled on those who are ceremonially unclean sanctify them so that they are outwardly clean. How much more, then, will the blood of Christ, who through the eternal Spirit offered himself unblemished to God, cleanse our consciences from acts that lead to death, so that we may serve the living God!*" (NIV).

Through the death of Jesus, we can come back into a relationship with God our Father, and we can have eternal life.

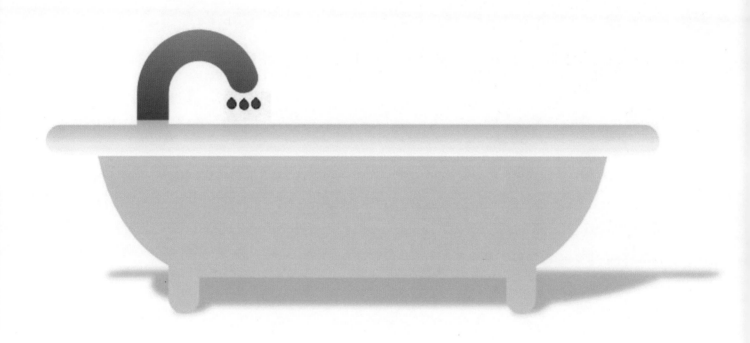

So, next time you find yourself asking the question, "*Why did Jesus have to die?*", it is because we sinned and deserved to die. We ourselves could not pay the price of sin because we are not perfect. Because Jesus is perfect, He was able to die in our place. He died so that our sins could be forgiven. If we believe that He died for us, we can have eternal life.

eternal life eternal life eternal life eternal life eternal life eternal life eternal life eternal life